UNDERSTANDING GOD'S PLAN

UNDERSTANDING GOD'S PLAN

Re-evaluating Your Relationship With God

TABITHA HENTON LAMB

CONTENTS

Introduction

he Place Called Process is based on a series of in-depth revelations inspired by the Holy Spirit. In essence it is a divine call to repentance and a re-examination of our stance with God. It is important that every Christian read it, and be reminded of our true purpose on earth. Many times we struggle to obey God, and even if we do, we do so partially in a way that still pleases a part of us. But God doesn't require partial worship. He doesn't want a selfish priesthood, but one drawn to Him in complete loyalty.

God loves us so much He created a special phase for those who still resist Him to teach them firmly, albeit lovingly, the importance of submission. This submission to His will is learned strictly through patience. If God doesn't "deal" with us, we will be pampered children – and what good is that when adversity strikes? Remember, the Lord disciplines those that He cherishes, and that particularly covers His Church, the body of Christ (Hebrews 12:6).

This book is examines the process of surrender. The first part draws you into divine revelations, and makes you ponder your life afresh. The next chapters take you through the relationship God has had with man from Biblical times to our present day, showing you the significance of obeying Him totally.

Reading this book will bless you with a new perspective on Grace, one that will encourage you to yield to the Spirit. If you have found yourself in a place of process, wait patiently until God's love is fully manifested, His glory fully sealed and His work fully completed in your life. Cheers!

The Place Called Process

I had a vivid dream. In this dream, I saw a man sitting in a small room that appeared to be in a hospital. Everything in the room was pure white. As he sat patiently on a chair, he had the posture of one who was waiting in complete surrender. He looked well and whole and you could see that his recovery was a complete one, as if he was waiting to be released.

On one of the top floors of this hospital, I saw another man. He was in a room lying on a bed wearing a hospital gown. I could see him connected to an IV and different types of machines. There was a plant sitting on a table next to him that had been given to him by a woman. This plant had tiny buds and a few leaves, even though it was really small. All of the man's attention was on this plant. He loved what this plant represented to him to the extent he was completely oblivious of where he was or what was about to transpire in his life. All he was focused on was this plant. He cherished the little fruit he saw. The value of this plant was not so much in the woman as it was in the gift itself, especially the buds and leaves.

As I wandered through the building, I walked into what looked like a huge auditorium. It was filled with thousands of people – I mean thousands! They were waiting for the man I had earlier seen seated on the chair in the hospital ward where everything was pure white. So, I went to look for him.

As I came off the elevator, I saw him now being wheeled from his room to the lowest level of this hospital, in what appeared to be a holding room in a discharge section. There I saw a number of well-known, celebrated preachers and pastors sitting in this room. Each of them was waiting for their number to be called to be discharged.

What was revealed to me was this. This hospital is a place where the lives of God's children are processed when they continue in disobedience or choose not to yield to His will.

I saw this operation in three phases: Admittance, Process and Discharge.

It started out with one man but then shifted to another to show me the operations of this place, which I will define as a place of "process."

Let us look at the first phase: Admittance.

Chapter Two

The First Phase: Admittance

Admittance is where the rebellious heart is still intact. This place is for those of us who are still not willing to come to the point of absolute surrender to the Will of God so we can receive the full release of the life of Christ in us. This phase occurs after many attempt to break through, only to circle back to the last failed test. The reason is disobedience in an area. This comes after a continuous cycle of repeats of places, circumstances or situations that may seem familiar.

The second man I saw was transported to this room almost as if angels were rerouting his path. He was admitted, given a room, provided garments, and toiletries. All he had there was the plant from the woman that he did not want to lose because he was attracted to the budding fruit.

"He that loses his life shall gain it," says Matthew 16:25. We can choose whether we want to lose our soul life (*psuche*) in this life or in the life to come. Our lives are routed to a place where great losses happen until we decide to empty ourselves completely and submit to God's will and plan for us. The place brings great sorrow and great loss in various dimensions and phases of our life; they could be in the area of health, finances, family, career, and so on until we come to a place of absolute surrender.

Submitting to God's will isn't as easy as it looks at times. The spirit may be willing, but the flesh is always weak. Whatever our spiritual man desires is usually contrary to the flesh, and whatever the flesh seeks, is contrary to what the spirit desires. This is because God's will may appear foolish, senseless or amusing to us, and our fleshly eyes find it difficult to see ourselves forever listening to God's instructions. These instructions may seem particularly foolish to the worldly wise, for 1 Corinthians 1:27 tells us, *"God hath chosen the foolish things of the world to confound the wise; and God hath chosen the weak things of the world to confound the things which are mighty."*

Here are a few things that make it difficult for Christians to yield completely to God or, even when they yield, do so partially:

1. Fear of the unknown

   We may doubt God's word about the future because we're yet to see it for ourselves. But it isn't in God's nature to reveal everything to us until a set time. When Abraham was asked by God to leave his father's house, he had no idea where God would lead him, or his descendants. Nevertheless, by faith he obeyed.

When Jesus asked Peter to let down his net after a night of no catch, Peter did so without hesitation. We should learn to trust God to lead us safely to the place of promise even if we have gone through much pain.

2. Pride

Believers struggling with the sin of pride are so much entangled with "self," they fail to give God the praise and adoration which is our due worship to Him. Somehow, they feel that their achievement is through their hard work alone, and sometimes push God into the background. So, when it comes to submission, they're the hardest to convince as they consider themselves self-sufficient. But if they refuse to yield, they will crash like King Nebuchadnezzar who lost his sanity for seven years, and was only restored when he acknowledged and submitted to the living God.

Pride is an impediment in our relationship with God. It blinds us to our true condition – our wretchedness without our Savior and the emptiness we experience when we continue to neglect Him. The proud have no place in heaven, and even in this life, God does not entertain them because they're in competition with Him.

Pride doesn't allow us to yield to God's will. Instead we rebel against His authority with consequences too dire to mention.

3. Shame

Sometimes yielding to God means abandoning certain habitual activities. God may ask you to renounce a particular lifestyle or habit, or social group or sometimes a job. Not conforming to the crowd could make us feel uncomfortable around our peers. We might be bothered by what people say; but what God says and thinks is paramount.

Disobedience may lead us into further trouble. King Saul is a perfect example of someone who often yielded to the pressure of others instead of yielding to God's instruction, and this cost him his throne.

In one situation, the Lord had asked that everything and everyone in Amalek should be destroyed, but in order to please his soldiers, he spared King Agag and the fattest of calves. God wasn't interested in his excuses and explanations, and immediately withdrew His presence from Him.

And Samuel said, Hath the LORD *as great delight in burnt offerings and sacrifices, as in obeying the voice of the* LORD? *Behold, to obey is better than sacrifice, and to hearken than the fat of rams.*

For rebellion is as the sin of witchcraft, and stubbornness is as iniquity and idolatry. Because thou hast rejected the word of the LORD, he hath also rejected thee from being king (1 Samuel 15:22-23).

When you continuously show God that your peers, family and colleagues are more important, you just have to remember that all those people could forsake you when things go wrong. Are they of greater worth than the God who died for you? They can abandon you but God is our very present help in trouble! (Psalm 46:1)

4. Loss of faith

Many times, after a tragedy or a disappointment, we tend to lose faith in our Maker. We ask questions like, "Why did my mama have to go?" "Why did I lose that job?" "I thought you loved me; I thought you would always be there for me?" "Why was I abused?" "Why did you abandon me in the dark?"

These questions are natural because of the hurt. But remember that the Holy Spirit's mission is to heal and bind those broken parts of you together. Again, total and lasting healing requires surrender.

Be comforted in the example of Job. Although he lost everything, he refused to renounce his faith in God. If you lose faith in God, then you're giving the devil an opportunity to say, "I told you, God, they're only serving You because it's comfortable for them. They don't really love You."

The purpose of certain painful circumstances is to test you, and often to help you grow. God has provided us with seasons. There's a time to mourn, and a time to celebrate. It was never meant to be rosy all the way. If it was, we would have remained in Eden. The only promise God has made is that if we surrender all our cares, He'll carry our burdens. So, cheer up, and pray for the Grace to be a faithful witness until the end.

So when we offer up ourselves, we agree to come willingly and embrace the afflictions He allows. When they are imposed upon us due to our disobedience, they come as blows to all phases of life. It is here that many will come to the point of **yielding** their heart and will to Him.

Take comfort that you are so precious in His sight that He has your days recorded in His book even before a single one had come to pass (Psalm 139:16).

I will now expand on the dream that God gave me to reveal this process as exemplified by the two men who were at two different phases of their lives. The first man was almost at the end of the process of complete surrender. He was now in a place of waiting, completely emptied out, only waiting on the will and timing of God for his life. You will find him empty as a shell as the emptying process is being carried out until he arrives at a state of perfection.

The second man was caught at the peak of his life and rerouted to this place. He was now waiting on the process and the start of his unknown journey into this realm.

It is my prayer we will come to identify where we are in life to allow a re-alignment in our thinking regarding God's strategy to mold and refine His sons.

So let us pray:

Dear Father, I pray we will come to see Your love and compassion in all this, to know the degree to which You will go to reveal everything in us that causes us to rebel against Your will, and to bring each one of us to the end of ourselves. I pray that illumination

will finally come to us through reve-
lation of Your word, in Jesus' name,
Amen.

THE SECOND PHASE: PROCESS

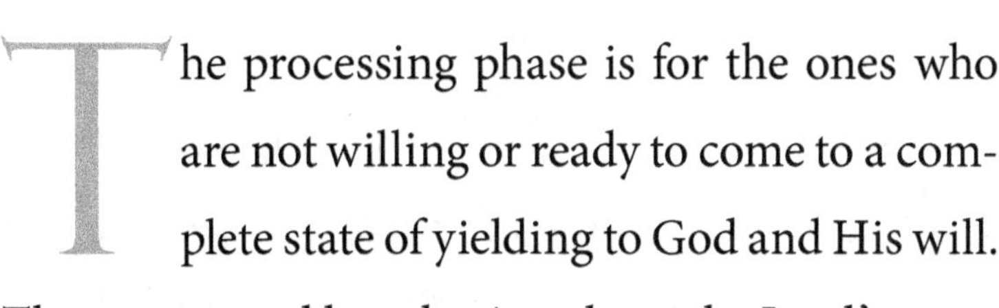

The processing phase is for the ones who are not willing or ready to come to a complete state of yielding to God and His will. They are routed here by Angels on the Lord's command (Hebrews 1:14).

The second man in my dream had no idea where he was or what was about to transpire in his life as he was set to undergo the beginning of the processing. It would involve great loss to his health, his wealth and all that had elevated him to his current status.

Processing, you see, involves crushing and the purpose of the crushing is to learn obedience. It is not until we have learned obedience that we are true sons of God. When we come through, we will walk in the manifested Power of God.

Obedience during crushing is equal to Power. If you see someone walking in Power, you know they have mastered the obedience learned through crushing.

Jesus told His disciples many things concerning His death for the sins of mankind. He accepted His destiny as the sacrificial Lamb; and yet, being human, He hesitated in the final hour. He had to bring the fleshly part of Himself into alignment with the will of God and to willingly drink the cup of suffering to appease the wrath of God for all mankind.

As His children by adoption, God wants the full-blown artistry of His handiwork to be made manifest in us. For this to happen, we must come to the point of agreement that we have no life outside of Him. Any life that we have outside of this is a counterfeit existence. The only valid life is the life

He lives through us. Say goodbye to even the heart, for it is no longer the seat of life. Only the life we chose to live through Christ counts.

Listen to the Father calling you: "My child, I want you to go where I send you. If you do not, you will be acting contrary to My will for you and I will make war with that life because it is Mine. Your life was never yours to begin with. It was Mine from eternity past. And it is Mine now and into eternity future. When you die, it's not the end – that is not the final hour but rather when you die to yourself. This is where Gethsemane enters your life to bring an utter end to your self life. When life hurts, it only hurts because you are not dead yet."

The issue is we live the wrong version of who we really are. Look at the ROI –return on our investment. For His great investment in you, return to Him whatever He asks, when He asks. The day that we live as our own possession must come to an end. Any place from this point forward will be who we were intended to become. We must agree and fall into the will of God, fall as an act of surrender. We must seek never to do life in our old un-renewed self again. That was an imposter. So let's be adventurous here. Come in and see what this new life is all about; come in to embrace the change by acceptance.

"Your strength comes when you do the will of you Father. The intensity is there in the crushing, the furnace of affliction. I have chosen, handpicked you to be crushed and broken in all areas. This is the threshing floor of your life, the place you are to come to after the plentiful harvest is collected. The fruit is here and its purpose is served in the pouring of the new wine after it is crushed, bruised, and battered."

When this process is complete, the person who now resides in you can endure anything and everything because he is not emotionally tied to the human heart, will, desires or appetites – only to the will of God. This is when the scope of your existence is brought into right perspective.

If you are ready and willing to be emptied, ask yourself these questions:

What do you still want to do in yourself?

What do you do that is of yourself?

What part of your will is still intact?

What doctrines are you still holding onto that are blocking your path?

What are you doing for self-glory?

Where in life is the will of the Father not enough?

Do I do what I do it to please me or to please Him?

What do I want to become of me?

What glory do I still seek and why do I seek it?

Why do I want or feel the need to have my own commandment or to speak on behalf of myself?

Jesus understood His purpose – He knew He came here to die. This is where we are missing it. We are so busy trying to live that we are totally missing the purpose. The purpose is to *die here* so that we can live with Him forever.

You may ask yourself why all of this is necessary and what purpose it will serve. The answer is that we come here to be legislators for God – to establish the Kingdom of God on earth. By being His legislators, we give Him access to the earth that He created for us. We are continuing in the steps of Jesus. Just as Jesus gave the Father access to mankind, so too does He give the children of God the tools to come into sonship with Him and bring many more sons with them. That means enforcing the authority over what God has already given us.

Luke 10:19:

> *Behold, I give unto you power to tread*
> *on serpents and scorpions, and over all*

the power of the enemy: and nothing

shall by any means hurt you.

Matthew 28:18-19:

And Jesus came and spake unto them,

saying, All power is given unto me in

heaven and in earth. Go ye therefore …

If Jesus has already given us all power and authority, Satan should not have dominion over the cosmos or the earth. By assuming that is the status quo, the church does not understand its true purpose. We should be training disciples into sonship so that we establish the Kingdom of God throughout all its generations, so there will be no end to His Kingdom.

Isaiah 9:7 defines the scope of this Kingdom:

Of the increase of his government and

peace there shall be no end, upon the

throne of David, and upon his king-

dom, to order it, and to establish it

*with judgment and with justice from
henceforth even for ever. The zeal of
the LORD of hosts will perform this.*

The zeal of the LORD makes such an unending government possible from generation to generation. To operate in Kingdom authority is to understand His Mission. Then we can operate in great power and authority. At base, we must come to a place of dying to our will in order to do the will of God. In the same way, we train up our children to assume kingdom authority, and our children's children in continuous succession.

As for our time here, all of our days are written in His book. We are either being led, rerouted in a waiting process, or being discharged into purpose. He has assigned Angels to guide us into our purpose. It is said when we deviate from our calling, the angels check the book and return to God for guidance and are instructed how to re-route us back on course.

When this process fails, we are shifted into process. We have no idea the sorrows and hardships that await the human soul because, as this phase begins, so begins the process of great loss. This correction happens when we do not give the right of way to the Holy Spirit and fail to offer a true surrender.

Whatever the phase we are in, know that the final outcome is for us to become the manifestation of the sons of God.

There are processes to surrendering to God. It starts with transitioning from Relationship to Grace. But, grace, mind you, is not license to sin – this is a misconception. We are done with the hyper grace teaching! No, grace is our ability to execute God's will: it is Power through Jesus Christ

Man must overcome the will just as Jesus did in the garden when He cried, "Father, not My will but Thine be done."

Mark 14:32-42:

And they came to a place which was named Gethsemane: and He saith to his disciples, sit ye here, while I shall pray. And He taketh with Him Peter and James and John, and began to be sore amazed, and to be very heavy; And saith unto them, My soul is exceeding sorrowful unto death: tarry ye here, and watch.

And He went forward a little, and fell on the ground, and prayed that, if it were possible, the hour might pass from Him. And He said, Abba, Father, all things are possible unto thee; take away this cup from Me: nevertheless, not what I will, but what thou wilt.

And He cometh, and finds them sleeping, and saith unto Peter, Simon, sleepiest thou? Could not thou watch one hour? Watch ye and pray, lest ye enter into temptation. The spirit truly is ready, but the flesh is weak. And again, He went away, and prayed, and spake the same words. And when He returned, He found them asleep again, (for their eyes were heavy,) neither wist they what to answer him.

And He cometh the third time, and saith unto them, Sleep on now, and take your rest: it is enough, the hour is come; behold, the Son of man is betrayed into the hands of sinners. Rise up, let us go; lo, he that betrayed me is at hand.

You have to stay in the darkness long enough to be processed or you will never know what was captured. Patience is the processing ward. It is here one is processed through and through inside and out so he can take possession of his soul. Be patient long enough to quiet and calm the soul.

Here are some of the likely issues we face at this time:

1. Fighting with God

    This occurs when God comes to you and asks you to do something and you respond with, "Who, me? Surely you are wrong, God?" We see this with Gideon as he argued with God from behind the winepress about his weakness. When God asked Moses to become His corporate spokesman and deliverer, Moses pointed to his speech impediment and lack of eloquence. In spite of all this, these great heroes were not zapped or disqualified by arguing with God, though a quick obedience might be better than struggling with God.

2. Counting the Cost

When God asks you to do what seems audacious, you need to take some time to consider the cost. Jesus tells us to consider if one of us wants to build a tower, wouldn't we first sit down and estimate the cost to see if we have enough money to complete it? (Luke 14:28) This isn't about questioning if God can do what He has asked you to do, but deciding if you are willing to pay the personal cost of accomplishing God's will.

3. Surrender

I know that the Bible tells us not to fear, but the things that God asks of us are often costly. If you've ever surrendered a relationship you cherished to the Lord, or a job, you might not have done it so easily.

Like love and forgiveness, surrender is a choice not an emotion. It's deciding to lay down your will and submit to God's will and desires. Clearly, God's will triumphs over every human understanding and must be accepted with deep reverence.

4. Overcoming Fear through Grace

Sometimes we surrender, but we can still be afraid of what God has asked us to do. It may be an area where we have to let go of control, or confront, or press past our fear, and step out and lead. Courage is not the absence of fear, but courage is pressing forward in spite of the fear. Grace is the aspect of God's love that covers our weaknesses; it will see you through the journey and not your own human effort.

It is not until my soul is quieted that I can see His love spring forth in the midst of the storm. It is then I can see His love chasing down my fears to overtake and overwhelm them. I can face and conquer my fears when I come to believe He is greater than the actual fear itself.

THE THIRD PHASE: WAITING

If you have found yourself in a place of process, just wait patiently. God's love will be fully manifested in your life, His glory will be fully sealed and His work completely finished.

Submission to His will is strictly learned through patience. Patience is more than a virtue: it's a fruit of the Holy Spirit (Galatians 5:22-23). Fruit are especially needed to withstand the trials of life including people who try us. The life of Jesus clearly illustrates this. Jesus was very patient with His disciples. They were sometimes thickheaded, lazy, selfish, and slow to comprehend. Even from a merely human standpoint, we can see how frustrating they must have been.

In spite of seeing the mighty miracles Jesus' worked and words of wisdom He spoke, they were often caught up in their own priorities – like which of them would be the greatest! They constantly wavered in their belief about who He really was. To say that was frustrating for Jesus would be an understatement. Yet do we find Him railing at His disciples over their foolishness and stupidity? Or making fun of them when they made mistakes?

But even more challenging at times is the patience that is God-directed. In every Christian's life there comes a time when one must wait upon God. Sometimes we must wait for a practical need to be met such as finding a job. At other times we must wait for a significant desire to find fulfillment, like finding a spouse or conceiving a child. And sometimes we wait for God to fulfill a promise, comfort us during a trial or assure us of forgiveness for some sin. In all these cases, we must be patient with God. This is a challenge because sometimes it's not clear whether it is God we're waiting for or for something in the natural to materialize.

Finally, Jesus exhibited patience with His Father as He waited for and worked towards the completion of His mission. Like David in the psalms, Jesus cried out in agony, offering His righteous pleas to God, even quoting scripture. This was not impatience but a way of heading off the temptation to be impatient by taking His complaint directly to God the Father.

What better example of patience to follow but our Lord, Jesus Christ!

DISCHARGE

The first man who surrendered no longer had anything anymore. All was left was an absolute surrender to God and His will. The man described here was broken and humbled in spirit, mind and heart. He had set his mind only to do the will of God from the inside out. The room was tiny and sparsely furnished – no décor, nothing fancy – so it looked completely white. He was sitting on a chair fully dressed, healthy and whole, in waiting mode.

This man was finally wheeled out from his room to the lower level of the hospital facility. He entered a huge auditorium within the facility, filled with other preachers and pastors. They had been through the same experience as him. Each of them had been broken and was now yielded to the will of God. They were all sitting patiently, formally dressed as if for a service or conference, as they waited for their number to be called.

As for the second man who looked at the plant in the second room on the top floor, this was the admittance level. This place has all of the fixtures – hospital bed, TV and all the comforts of a hospital that you can imagine. The Lord revealed to me this is a place of process to which we are carefully guided when we refuse to yield to His will and plan. This process brings about great loss and sorrow in the life of the rebellious. Its purpose and design is to bring us to a place of total surrender to the will to God.

The final phase was the discharge room which led to the auditorium. All the occupants in this room had been broken and humbled, and were ready to receive their assignment.

This dream is what moved me to write this book.

One of the unique things about the God we serve is that He is a God of times and seasons. This proves that He operates in a systematic and orderly manner. And He also expects that of His children, so we shouldn't only seek to understand everything, but to be patient while He perfects everything that concerns us.

The creation story in the Book of Genesis, Chapter 1 provides concrete evidence that God Himself follows a process. It would have been possible for Him to "cough" out a perfect world for mankind even in a minute. However, He used seven days to complete His creation. Sadly, we enjoy reading the story but fail to learn deep lessons from it. The main lesson is the value of timing and process. God wants us to be patient while He works through our lives. The fruit of patience is to there to build mature and dependable children who can withstand whatever storms come their way.

Without learning the beauty of patience which enables us to surrender all to Him, we will never come to understand the depth of his love. God always knows better than we do, or think. For this reason, He demands complete submission manifested in our obedience to reach the point He has promised to take us to. If He did not exempt His Son from this principle, we too must follow the footsteps of the greatest example of all, our Lord Jesus Christ.

It is written of Jesus in Hebrews 5:8-10,

> *Though he was a son, yet learned he obedience by the things he suffered, and once made perfect, became the source of eternal salvation unto all of them that obey him!*

This verse teaches us two important things. First, we learn obedience from suffering. If we have everything easy, we're never going to grow and mature as Christians. Tough times create tough people, and tough people last longer than those who have it easy.

Second, suffering humbles us: it breaks our hardened hearts and makes us vulnerable. It is at this point that we're expected to surrender totally, but for some reason, many Christians love to push through on their own because they feel they have options. There is a difference between suffering alone, and suffering with God alongside you. With God with you, He will sustain you.

On the cross, Jesus still held on to His Father, clinging to every word of His promise. All along He still had the ability to exercise His power of choice until He cried out, *"It is finished,"* bowed His head and gave up His spirit (John 19:30). Remember how He had earlier struggled with the will of the Father, but now was completely surrendered?

In the garden of Gethsemane, Jesus went through a human moment at the thought about the suffering that awaited Him, and He prayed for His Father to reconsider the cup He was about to drink. But in the end, He surrendered to the will of the Father as an obedient Son!

Walking with God doesn't require options on the side or partial obedience. One must be ready to give up everything including one's life. Why? God loves us so much and would give us anything that we ask. Already He gave us His Son. But He has to know how sincere your heart is, how much you love Him and care about Him. Sometimes, some tests could be weightier than others, but in everything you pass through, He always gives you the grace to endure.

So the place called process dwells on God's timing, rules and principles. The longer you resist His will, the tougher the journey, until you come on bended knee and acknowledge that without God, you're nothing, and He is indeed your Lord and Master. He is worthy of your worship, honesty, devotion, obedience.

Obedience is an act of Worship. Far from being a routine reverence or the singing of beautifully written songs… worship is a deep acknowledgment that comes from a broken spirit, one that realizes that man is just dust, yet God is so mindful of Him. How wonderful that is!

But the Jews of old were stuck in their routine religiosity, and couldn't fathom the mystery of worship. That was the reason they always failed God by resisting Him. If God demands obedience, He isn't confused or mincing words: it is obedience He wants and not sacrifice. Jesus stressed the importance of worship to the woman of Samaria; that a time would come when people would No Longer Need Mountains or Sacred Buildings to worship God, but they would worship Him in Spirit and in truth! (John 4:21-24). When this happens, the veil is torn, and we have the Law of His glorious love written and sealed upon their hearts (Galatians 6:2).

Everyone is created for a purpose. But to reach the peak, we must let God rule. When we reject His guidance, we're asking for trouble. If God neglects us, it becomes worse. But if He's patient enough to take us through the place of process, we just have to let go of every material or physical thing that stands in the way of us and Him.

The process of teaching us to submit is usually worse for the rebellious as we see in the children of Israel suffering needlessly in the desert for forty years until a godly generation that reverenced God arose. It was their impatience and hardness of heart that led them into fashioning the golden calf when Moses was on the mountain communing with God. The same rebellious spirit pushed them to grumble and murmur against God, forgetting all of His benefits...and they paid the price for it!

If only they'd been wise to learn from their ancestor Abraham, who made preparations to offer his only son to God! Or Joseph, who could have upgraded his lot in life by succumbing to the seductions of the mistress of the household! But these men understood that the whole purpose of man is to serve God, and the greatest service is submission.

How do I know if I am there? You know that when you find yourself on a road that is so familiar you are no longer operating from a conscious mindset but one you have internalized in your day-to-day routine. Now you can now complete your journey effortlessly. That's grace.

Matthew 16:25:

> *For whosoever will save his life shall*
> *lose it: and whosoever will lose his life*
> *for My sake shall find it.*

THE SIGNIFICANCE OF PROCESS

Let us examine the attributes of the word "process." What are its parts and what is its purpose?

Purpose is the reason for which something is done, exists or is created for. Further defined, it means to set as one's intention or objective.

God has allowed suffering, even purposed it.

When our wills are contrary to His will, He will bring us back to His will.

So what is the purpose of this strategy called process? It is intended to bring us to the end of ourselves. This is designed to get us to the purest form of who we are. All of what has shaped us has to be removed for our lives for us to come into alignment with the true version of ourselves. It is not until we are empty that He can fill us.

If we can yield to God fully in our lives, then we will enjoy life to the full, to overflowing. When you were born again, your spirit was immersed in the nature and life of God in Christ. "If this is true, then why do I not experience an outward life that is even close to the life Jesus lived on earth?" you ask. "Why do believers, differ outwardly in their daily experiences?"

The answer is found in the command of these three words: "Yield to God." What does it mean to "Yield to God?" The Amplified version is very informative about this,

> *Do not go on offering members of your body to sin as instruments of wicked-ness. But offer yourselves to God [in a decisive act] …* (Romans 6:13)

God lives inside of us as believers. But we must yield ourselves to him in a decisive act. The degree to which we yield ourselves to Him determines how much of Him will be revealed and manifested outwardly.

We all know how to yield, except that it was mostly yielding to sin. Before we met the Lord, we yielded our bodies to sin: our mouths for lying, our hands for stealing, our bodies for sexual impurity, and so on.

Whenever we allow our bodies to be used for something, we are yielding to it. God wants you to yield, or present, your bodies to Him as a living sacrifice (Romans 12:1). It is a decision to relinquish control of your life to Him as Lord. You will be so grateful you did, because it is in that place that you will enjoy life to the fullest.

So, do not think it strange that you're going through fiery trials. James 1:2-4, admonishes us to count it all joy when we fall into diverse temptations "*knowing this, the trying of our faith worketh patience.*" So let patience have *her* perfect work, that we may be perfect and entire, wanting nothing.

He is here with us, to dress and to adorn us to fit us for our function: to be a model for His Glory, and for His Kingdom.

ELEMENTS OF TEMPTATION AND TRIALS

What is temptation? Temptation is a seduction to evil, a solicitation to do wrong. The motive behind temptation is always to deceive and to lead man unconsciously into sin to ruin him. Temptation is the tempter looking through the keyhole into the room where we are living, while sin is the drawing back the bolt and making it possible for him to enter.

There are several steps in temptation: enticement, through weakening the will; strong imagination, by entertaining lust and taking delight in viewing; conceiving lust by yielding; sin in committing the sinful act. And, finally, there is death in suffering the consequences of actual sin (John 6:23).

Temptation in itself is not sin; in fact, to a believer, it is the call to battle. The point is we are in a continual war against our soul, and it is not simply a momentary skirmish. Our flesh, the evil world system and the evil one is resolutely determined to take us down – "to devour" us!

We may think of sin as a single act, but God sees it as the initiator of a process. Adam committed one act of sin, and yet that one act brought sin, death, and judgment on the whole human race. James described this process of sin in four stages: Desire, Deception, Disobedience, and Death.

James gives us a strategy for overcoming the deadly lure of temptation: we must first recognize its source, its force and its course. The flesh is the source, and its nature is evil.

We begin on the understanding that every man is tempted. James 1:14 says: "*...every man is tempted, when he is drawn away of his own lust, and enticed.*" We must stop being deceived regarding this strategic truth, lest we are swept downstream unaware of the strong pull of the temptation that comes from within. See, we are drawn away and enticed by what is already in us – this propensity, this vulnerability or unresolved issue. (To clarify further, no one else is to blame for this but me.) Then when what is in me (lust) has conceived, this particular lust brings forth sin: and sin, when it is finished, brings forth death (James 1:13-15). Do not fall into the error of believing that temptation is purely external, my beloved brothers and sisters. It preys on what is within.

But even temptation has its limits as 1 Corinthians 10:13 goes on to explain. God does not allow temptation beyond our capacity to endure and He always makes an escape route so that we will not be tempted beyond our ability to withstand:

> *There hath no temptation taken you*
> *but such as is common to man: but*
> *God is faithful, who will not suffer you*

to be tempted above that ye are able;
but will with the temptation also make
a way to escape, that ye may be able to
bear it.

His Spirit will support us in standing firm in the midst of temptation as long as our focus is set on Him.

Now temptation must be distinguished from trials. While temptation is a seduction to evil, a trial or test aims at a man's good, making him conscious of his true moral self. God tries men but the motive of a trial differs from that of a temptation. In a temptation it is the devil that induces man to do wrong. But God tries men to bring out the best in them, that they may find out their weaknesses and be saved from doing wrong. God never causes a heart to be inclined towards evil.

Let no man say when he is tempted, I
am tempted of God: for God cannot be

tempted with evil, neither tempteth he
any man (James 1:13).

So what is a Trial? A trial is a kind of test to put to proof, to examine, and question the moral caliber of a man and the soundness of his faith. The man who stands true in them proves his doctrines sound, his faith genuine and his character unimpeachable. Moreover, tests work patience and patience works perfection: personal perfection in the knowledge of the gospel and the will of God, personal completeness in all graces and gifts of God.

> *Knowing this, that* the *trying of your*
> *faith worketh patience.* But *let patience*
> *have her perfect work, that ye may be*
> *perfect and entire, wanting nothing*
> (James 1:3-4).

Watch the beautiful portrait He will paint of our lives after we have been tried. We are in the hand of God and all stakes are on Him. The eye of the beholder is on Him, the One who sees and knows all things. Nothing is hidden from our Sovereign God. To allow us to see His plan at work in our lives, He has to bring us out because here His Word is at stake! Here All dependency must be upon Him. He will lead and to guide us carefully through the surgery of pain. He will navigate us with great tenderness into all that He has for us.

Our Christian journey begins with accepting Jesus Christ as our Lord and Savior. Jesus, the Lord of our lives, is the one who controls and rules the course of our lives. We surrender to His Lordship when we get to the point that we have made up our minds to do what He wants instead of what we want. This is the most important decision any human being can ever make. It was the decision that got you born again, and it is that decision that will make you abundantly fruitful on earth. Everything else you will enjoy with God comes after these moments of surrender.

God wants you to love Him to the point that you want to please Him and do what He wants. He does not want you to surrender to Him out of fear, but out of love.

> *There is no fear in love; but perfect love casteth out fear: because fear hath torment. He that feareth is not made perfect in love* (1John. 4:18).

Do you love the Lord? If you do, you will want to please Him. You please Him by doing what He commands. He is infinitely wiser than you, and His commands for you will make your life sweet and not bitter! Sometimes, doing what He wants may seem to be against what you think is good for you. This is where Lordship comes in. You surrender by your spontaneous act of love.

The day you make this decision in your heart, as a Christian, to love God truly, you will set your life on a glorious path forever. Many believers go ahead living their lives the way they want and wonder why things such as sin, Satan, or even poverty and disease are Lording it over them. The Lordship of Christ is your protection from other lords. He will never hurt you. Your life will only become sweeter!

The suffering and the trials position us to be empty so we can be filled. This process works best when there is much brokenness and despair of one's soul. Jesus said in the garden, *"My soul is exceedingly sorrowful even unto death"* (Mark 14:34). The strength came in the surrender.

Jesus never lost sight of His purpose. He knew it was the cup that was prepared for Him. But in the garden Jesus, out of human emotion, prays a human prayer to release Him from the cup: *"Abba, Father, all things are possible unto thee; take away this cup from me: nevertheless not what I will, but what thou wilt"* (Mark 14:36). He acknowledged there was nothing too difficult for God and that the Father could allow the cup to pass from Him.

So He petitioned the Father to do just this and God said nothing.

He was God and if He willed for the course to be different, then the new will would come into effect However, Jesus recognized it was His human will inserting itself; at first undetected and dormant, now it was crying out. Now it had to die in order for Him to surrender to the will of the Father. The garden was the test of His soul. But the Son ultimately surrenders His human will to the divine will of the Father.

Here He submitted His will to be in sync with the will of God all the way to the time of His final crushing, for it is at the prospect of crushing that we typically fall away. If Jesus had not intentionally died to His will, He would not have made it to the cross.

Jesus differed from Moses who could not yield the part of himself that was inadequate and defective over to God. His underlying judgmental attitude led him to disobey God's express command. Numbers 20 describes how when they lacked water in the wilderness, and the people complained (yet again!), God asked Moses to speak to the rock. But rather than speak to the rock, Moses actually struck the rock twice and spoke to the people, *"Hear now, ye rebels; must we fetch you water out of this rock?"* (verse 10)

Yes, the miracle happened and water gushed out from the rock. But Moses had misrepresented the God of mercy to the people, and this was his penalty:

> *And the* LORD *spake unto Moses and Aaron, Because ye believed me not, to sanctify me in the eyes of the children of Israel, therefore ye shall not bring this congregation into the land which I have given them* (Numbers 20:12).

The one who made the mouth is well able to cause it to speak according to the creator's intent and design. You take every inadequacy in your life and place it before God. It is not for you to hold but for you to give up. "Thy will be done, the will for which I was sent into the world." This is what Jesus uttered.

Jesus had to die to the part of the will in Him that still remained. He had faced death on multiple occasions before, but this had never caused a desire to petition God to change His will concerning Him. The time of crushing will draw out the finest molecule of what is in us. You see, even though He was designed for the will of God, He still had to be proven.

Who in the days of his flesh, when he had offered up prayers and supplications with strong crying and tears unto him that was able to save him from death, and was heard in that he feared; Though he were a Son, yet learned he

> *obedience by the things which he suf-*
> *fered...* (Hebrews 5:7-8)

And now He is seated in a place of highest honor and power at the right hand of God (Ephesians 1:20-22).

Everything that could cause a hindrance to the will of God was dealt with in the garden. The crushing of the will brought total obedience to God, a complete pulverizing of it to the finest molecule which brought it to the ultimate act of obedience.

He had to be tested before He came to this magnitude of Power. To ensure not one human particle remained in Him. He suffered Himself to be crushed and, in this crushing, He learned obedience. He offered Himself up when He said, "Nevertheless if I must take it, I will. Not My will but Thine be done." The cup, the crushing of the soul, the will of man, the part of man that caused Him to go contrary to the will of God had to be dealt with. The soul of man was in that cup – Adam came to disobedience here – but Jesus came to complete obedience.

It is not until the will of man was emptied out that Jesus was strengthened within Him. The strengthening afforded Him what was needed to cause Him to endure what was ahead of Him. He was a dead man walking. The feelings, emotions, desires, appetites, all tied to the soul, were in sub-jugation. It is here that the claim of the human will, with its intents, motives, actions and its deeds, was negated. When you have no will you have no fleshly desires or appetites, no feelings, no emo-tions, no concerns of your own. It is from this place of emptying that He fulfilled the will of God in the final lap of his race.

Luke 5:38 tells us that new wine must be put into new wineskins lest it expands and breaks the old wineskins. When there are new wineskins both wine and skins are preserved. You cannot fill a vessel that is already at a full capacity or cannot contain the effervescence of the new wine that is being poured into it. In the same way Jesus had to be emptied of the human will (old wineskin) so as to be filled with the will of God (new wineskin). He had to endure the cross but also to come to realize the magnitude of the Power of God.

Can you stand being emptied?

Conclusion

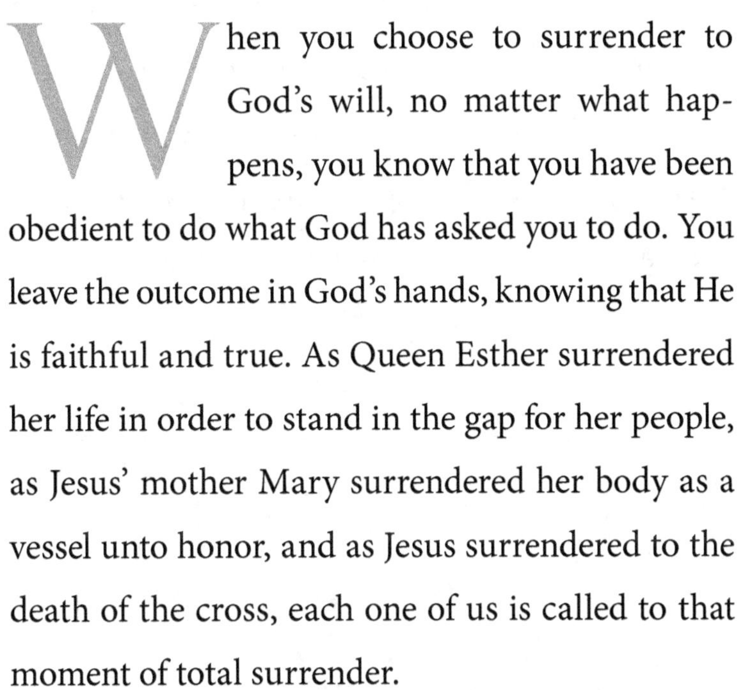

When you choose to surrender to God's will, no matter what happens, you know that you have been obedient to do what God has asked you to do. You leave the outcome in God's hands, knowing that He is faithful and true. As Queen Esther surrendered her life in order to stand in the gap for her people, as Jesus' mother Mary surrendered her body as a vessel unto honor, and as Jesus surrendered to the death of the cross, each one of us is called to that moment of total surrender.

A deliberate decision to study this book would help you understand that man is nothing by himself: man was created for surrendering. For surrender is the only way to show faith in God, and what is faith without obedience? When you decide to surrender to God, it may be costly, but in the end there are glorious rewards.

True surrender is not simply surrender of our external circumstances but surrender of our will – and once that is done, the surrender is complete. The greatest crisis we ever face is the surrender of our will. Yet God never forces a person's will into surrender. He never begs. He patiently waits until the person willingly gives it all over to Him.

NOTES

NOTES

Notes

Notes

NOTES

NOTES

NOTES

Notes

NOTES